Holidays

Von alexandria kom ich har gefarn
Vnd bringe vil gúter wår die weil ich inh
sparn Ich wil sie gebe vmb kleines gelt
recht vnd got liepst ich da mit vel ongelt

BY BERNICE BURNETT
(REVISED EDITION)

FRANKLIN WATTS, INC.
NEW YORK | 1974

THE FIRST BOOK OF

Holidays

Frontispiece: one of the earliest holiday greeting cards to survive today is a woodcut printed around 1450 in the Rhine Valley, Germany. Its message reads: "Here I come from Alexandria and bring many good years to give generously. I will give them for almost no money and have only God's love for my reward."

Cover design: George MacLain

Library of Congress Cataloging in Publication Data

Burnett, Bernice.
    The first book of holidays.

    SUMMARY: Describes the origins and ceremonies of the major holidays observed in the United States and some of those observed in other parts of the world.
    Bibliography: p.
    1. Holidays—Juvenile literature. [1. Holidays]
I. Title.
GT3932.B86   1974   394.2'6   74–3075
ISBN 0–531–00548–8

Contents

Traditional Holidays and National Observances

Sometimes when you wake up in the morning—even before you open your eyes to see if it is sunny or rainy—you know that the day is special. "Something is going to happen today," you say, "something wonderful! Today's a holiday!"

Most holidays are days that are set aside for rest or play, to help remember something important that happened, or to honor some great person. Other holidays are days that used to have real meaning in our lives but that have been almost forgotten. Often we still celebrate the traditions that are connected with them.

Many of our most important holidays are *religious holidays*. The holiday that Americans observe most often is a religious one, the Sabbath. It is a holy day that is set aside as a day of worship and rest. (The word "holiday" was once "holy day.") Christians keep the Sabbath on Sunday and Jews celebrate it on Saturday.

National holidays are days that all the people in a country want to remember. The Congress of the United States has set aside certain legal public holidays for national observance. New holidays are added from time to time by acts of Congress, and sometimes the dates of observance of holidays are changed. Recent changes were made by an act of Congress on June 24, 1968, which became effective on January 1, 1971. These are the legal public holidays and the dates of their observance according to this act:

New Year's Day, January 1.
Washington's Birthday, the third Monday in February.
Memorial Day, the last Monday in May.
Independence Day, July 4.
Labor Day, the first Monday in September.
Columbus Day, the second Monday in October.
Veterans Day, the fourth Monday in October.
Thanksgiving Day, the fourth Thursday in November.
Christmas Day, December 25.

Many state legislatures have enacted laws to make their states' observances conform to the dates set by the Federal Congress.

Inauguration Day, the day when the newly elected president of the United States takes office, is also a legal public holiday. It takes place on January 20 every four years, because the president is chosen by our people every fourth year.

In addition to these holidays the president may announce or proclaim that a certain day is to be celebrated as a national holiday. For example, after our astronauts landed on the moon, President Nixon proclaimed July 31, 1969, as a National Day of Participation, so that all of our people could share in the pride and joy of that historic achievement.

Governors of states also may proclaim days of celebration in their own states.

Regional holidays are days that are celebrated in a particular part of the country. In Maine and Massachusetts, for instance, the third Monday in April is a holiday—Patriots' Day. The Revolutionary War patriots are especially honored in these two New England states.

Another kind of holiday is a *family holiday*. These are personal occasions such as birthdays or anniversaries.

NEW YEAR'S DAY

An old Roman god with two faces—one for looking forward to the new year and the other for looking back at the old—may seem to have nothing at all to do with Americans today. But we follow the custom of staying up late on December 31 to watch the old year out and the new year in because of Janus, the Roman god of beginnings and endings and openings and closings.

It was Julius Caesar, the Roman emperor, who decided that the year should start in the month he named January in honor of Janus. Before Caesar's time, Romans celebrated the New Year when spring came. But the men who studied the stars and the sun to work out Caesar's calendar made the year too long. In 1582, Pope Gregory XIII changed the calendar to the one we use today. In the change, New Year's Day was moved from January 14, Janus's festival day, to January 1.

The New Year's Eve customs of making noise—blowing horns or whistles and ringing bells—and wearing costumes or silly hats probably go back to the Roman midwinter festival.

New Year's Day itself is a legal holiday all over the United States. Since it is a day of beginnings, many people like to begin new programs or stop old habits. And they like to have parties and exchange good wishes for the coming year with their friends.

LINCOLN'S BIRTHDAY

Abraham Lincoln's birthday on February 12 is celebrated as a legal holiday in most northern and western states. It is not observed in some southern states.

Lincoln was the sixteenth president of the United States. During his term in office the only war that ever divided our country—the Civil War, or the War Between the States—was fought. Although some of the southern states had wanted to leave the United States and form a country of their own, the Union was preserved under the leadership of President Abraham Lincoln.

Many of the southern states pay tribute to the memory of Robert E. Lee, commander of the Confederate armies during the Civil War, on January 19, which is a legal holiday in twelve states, and to the memory of Jefferson Davis, president of the Confederacy, on June 3.

Above: Abraham Lincoln's address at Gettysburg, the battle site of a decisive Union victory during the Civil War, is an eloquent and memorable statement of the American ideals of liberty and equality.

Below: portrait of Abraham Lincoln shortly before his assassination.

These ornate paper lace valentines made
around 1880 are typical of the
lavish style of the cards of that period.

SAINT VALENTINE'S DAY

Everybody knows that Valentine's Day is a special day for sweethearts, but nobody knows exactly why people first came to celebrate it. And, over the years, many different stories have grown up about how this very old holiday came to be.

The most common myth about Saint Valentine's Day says that it is celebrated in memory of two Roman martyrs named Valentine who lived long ago. When the Romans became Christians, the church made them stop celebrating a rough and noisy festival, called the *Lupercalia,* which fell on February 15. Saint Valentine's Day, in honor of the two Valentines, took its place and was observed a day earlier.

Much later people sent messages and good wishes to each other by mail on this holiday and these came to be called valentines. Today children often carry pretty paper valentines to school and stuff them into valentine boxes for their friends. Though children have fun on Saint Valentine's Day, it really is a day for sweethearts.

Saint Valentine's Day is not a legal holiday in any of the states, but is a traditional one.

SAINT PATRICK'S DAY

This holiday honors St. Patrick, the patron saint of Ireland. Americans of Irish descent and of many other national origins celebrate Saint Patrick's Day on March 17. They march in parades, gather together for big dinners, dance Irish jigs, and sing Irish songs.

Saint Patrick's Day parades are held in many cities. People wear something green in memory of Ireland, the Emerald Isle. Some wear shamrocks, which are like little three-leaved clovers.

St. Patrick was born in Scotland in about the year 389. He went to Europe to study religion and to become a priest and a bishop, and returned to Ireland to teach the people about the God he believed in. We celebrate the anniversary of his death in 493 as Saint Patrick's Day.

There are many wonderful stories about St. Patrick. The most famous is that he drove the snakes out of Ireland. This is only a legend, but the Irish will tell you that you cannot find a snake in the whole of Ireland.

EASTER

For Christians, Easter is a day of great gladness, since it celebrates the time when Jesus Christ rose from the dead. Most Christian churches teach that because of this all people who believe in Christ will have everlasting life.

Easter is one of the greatest religious festivals of the year. For a long time, during the early days of the Christian church, it was celebrated on different dates. But in the year 325 a council of churchmen met at a town called Nicaea and fixed the date for Easter as the first Sunday following the first full moon after March 21.

In many churches the celebration begins about forty days before Easter Sunday, on Ash Wednesday. The period until Easter is called Lent, an old word meaning "spring." Lent is celebrated in memory of the forty days that Jesus spent praying alone in the wilderness before He went out to teach and help people. During Lent many people make sacrifices such as giving up some of the things they like to do or not eating certain foods they enjoy.

The Sunday before Easter is called Palm Sunday, in memory of a journey Jesus made into the city of Jerusalem. People along the way covered the path before him with palm branches, and many churches today commemorate this event on Palm Sunday by giving palm branches to those in church.

In the week before Easter are two very important holidays—Holy Thursday and Good Friday. Holy Thursday is celebrated in memory of Christ's last supper with His disciples. Good Friday is a sad day. It marks the time when Christ died on the cross on the hill at Calvary. Church altars are left bare, and candles are unlighted. Only solemn music is played. Sometimes churches are draped with black cloth.

On Easter Sunday the Lenten period of sorrow and fasting ends. Church altars are decorated with beautiful Easter lilies. Candles are lighted again. Church services celebrate the day that Christ rose from the dead. Sometimes all the members of a church go up high on a hill to hold sunrise services on Easter morning. Large crosses marking these places can be seen against the sky for many miles.

Although Easter is a religious holiday, we still follow customs that go back to an ancient festival that was held at this time of year long before Christianity. At this season the ancient Anglo-Saxon people used to have a festival in honor of Eostre, their goddess of light and spring. Her name has come down as the English name of the Christian holiday.

One of the old customs that comes from early times is coloring Easter eggs. Colored eggs were used in the spring celebrations of the ancient Persians, Egyptians, Greeks, and Romans. You may think that the celebration of the belief in everlasting life is very far indeed from celebrating Easter with prettily decorated eggs. But it is not so strange as it seems, for the egg holds within itself the beginning of new life.

APRIL FOOL'S DAY

If anyone were to wish you a Happy New Year on April 1, you would be sure he was playing an April Fool's joke. But April Fool's Day started in France, some scholars believe, just because April 1 once *was* New Year's Day. When the king of France adopted the calendar that is used today, and the new year began on January 1, many people forgot or did not like the new date. They were called April fools.

Frenchmen used to exchange gifts with their friends on April 1 when that date began the year. They kept the custom of sending gifts on that date. But after the change in the calendar the kinds of gifts changed, too. People started to send silly or worthless gifts, or packages made to look like something they were not.

That is one explanation for this holiday. But another explanation may be that this lighthearted festival is in honor of spring.

PAN AMERICAN DAY

Our own country and twenty-three other American republics observe Pan American Day each year on April 14. Pan American Day is the anniversary of the creation in 1890 of the Pan American Union, made up of the nations of South, Central, and North America.

Some of the American countries began holding conferences as early as 1826 with the aim of forming friendships. The First International Conference of American States, which included all the independent nations in this hemisphere, was held in Washington, D.C., in 1889.

We have celebrated Pan American Day since 1931. There are ceremonies in the Pan American Building in Washington, D.C., which flies the flags of all the Pan American nations. Schools and interested groups present programs showing the ways in which the Pan American countries are working together to help each other.

ARBOR DAY

The first Arbor Day was started by a man named J. Sterling Morton in 1872. He noticed that the soil of the treeless plains of Nebraska, where he lived, was getting drier and was blowing away. He made up his mind to do everything he could to restore the earth's richness. The best way to do this, he believed, was to plant trees. After much talking he convinced the people of Nebraska that a tree-planting day should be established.

More than a million trees were planted in Nebraska the first year, and it became known as the Tree Planters' State. Morton is called the Father of Arbor Day. Nebraska celebrates Arbor Day each year on his birthday, April 22.

Other states soon followed Nebraska's example, and now every state in the Union except Alaska celebrates this day on various dates. Most observe it in April. Where there is not a fixed date, the governors of the states proclaim a certain day as Arbor Day.

LAW DAY

A holiday that was designed to help us to recognize how important laws are in our country is Law Day, observed on May 1. Law Day was first proclaimed in 1958 by President Dwight D. Eisenhower. The first official observance was in 1961 when Congress established Law Day as an official holiday. Schools, law associations, and some courts observe Law Day with programs about how the courts operate, how foreign-born persons become citizens, how the laws are made, how they are enforced, and how justice is administered.

MOTHER'S DAY

A special day for mothers is rather a new holiday in our country. In 1914, Congress asked the president of the United States to proclaim Mother's Day as a day to be remembered throughout the nation.

Miss Anna Jarvis of Philadelphia is known as the founder of Mother's Day, for she spent her life trying to make sure that one day a year would be set aside to honor mothers. It was Anna Jarvis who started the custom of wearing a flower on Mother's Day. And now many people wear a red rose or a pink carnation on that day if their mother is living or a white flower if she is dead.

MAY DAY

Holiday traditions change. New holidays are born and old ones die out. May Day is one of the holidays that has almost disappeared. Today very little is left to remind us of what May Day used to be like.

Scholars who study ancient customs believe that May Day customs go back to an old Roman holiday celebrating the blossoming of flowers. In some places in our own country, people still deliver May baskets. Children visit their friends' houses early in the morning or at twilight, without being seen, and leave fancy little

baskets filled with pretty spring flowers on the doorsteps. In Rome, people used to make similar offerings of flowers to statues of Flora, the goddess of flowers.

Certain schools still celebrate May Day. Some choose an especially pretty girl to be queen of the May and rule over the festival. They wind a long pole, called a maypole, with ribbons, and decorate it with flowers. Then they stand it upright on the lawn and dance about it, weaving in and out with ribbons that hang from its top, until it is striped with colored ribbons.

MEMORIAL DAY

Memorial Day is a holiday that is not a celebration. It is the saddest of all days for our country, for it is in memory of the hundreds of thousands of our men who have been killed in war.

This day used to be called Decoration Day, and sometimes it still is so called. It is the day when families and friends decorate the graves of soldiers with flags and wreaths of flowers.

Memorial Day began to be observed soon after the Civil War ended. The war that divided our country was terrible and bitter. But today both the North and the South are proud that our nation is united.

Northern states honor their dead on a day in late May. In the past this day was May 30, but most states have changed the date of this observance to the last Monday in May.

In the South many states also observe another Memorial Day called Confederate Memorial Day, in memory of the soldiers who fought in the Confederate Army during the War Between the States.

In former times, May Day was an important holiday and
the festivities lasted all day long. The holiday marks
the arrival of the new growing season and probably
has its roots in ancient agricultural and fertility rites.

The dates on which Confederate Memorial Day is observed in these states are:

Alabama, fourth Monday in April.

Arkansas, the Sunday closest to April 26.

Florida, April 26.

Georgia, April 26.

Kentucky, June 3.

Louisiana, June 3.

Maryland, May 30.

Mississippi, fourth Monday in April.

North Carolina, May 10.

South Carolina, May 10.

Tennessee, June 3.

FATHER'S DAY

Fathers have their own special holiday every year on the third Sunday in June. In order to show them how much they are loved all year round, on that day their children and grandchildren write them notes, send them greeting cards, and give them presents.

Father's Day is not an official holiday, and it has not been widely celebrated for very long. The idea of having such a holiday is believed to have started with Mrs. John Bruce Dodd of Spokane, Washington, who wanted to honor her own father. The first public celebration of Father's Day took place in Spokane on the third Sunday in June, 1910. Everyone who went to church was asked to wear a red rose if his father was living, or a white one if he was dead. Other celebrations were held from time to time in various places throughout the country, and now the day is celebrated each year.

FLAG DAY

Each year, June 14 is set aside as a day to honor our flag. On that day the red, white, and blue banner flies from all public buildings and from many homes and stores.

When the colonies declared their independence from Great Britain they wanted a flag to be the symbol of the young nation. Flag Day is the anniversary of the day the first flag was adopted in 1777 by the Continental Congress.

Each year, on June 14, celebrations
honoring the flag are held all over
the United States. The happy
children above are participating
in a Flag Day ceremony in
midtown Manhattan, New York City.

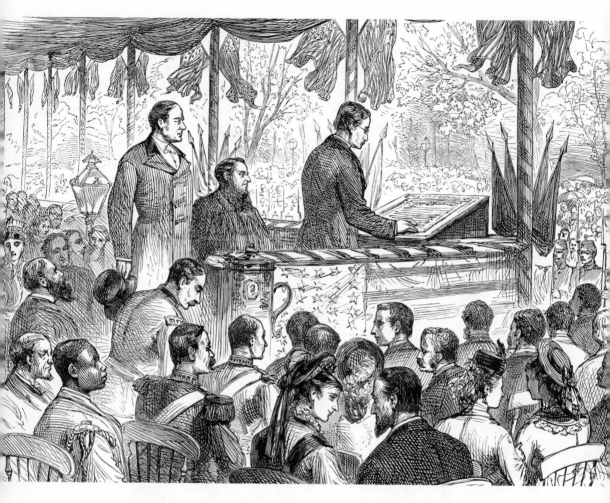

On July 4, 1776, John Hancock, president
of the Continental Congress, signed the
Declaration of Independence and made its
adoption official. Although the resolution
for independence from England was passed
by Congress on July 2, most members did not
actually sign the document until a month later.

INDEPENDENCE DAY

In the steeple of the State House of an eastern city a great bell rang out one day in 1776, summoning the people to meet in the town square to hear the reading of a document.

The city was Philadelphia. The meeting place was what is now called Independence Square. The bell was the famous Liberty Bell. The document was the Declaration of Independence, which announced the American colonies' freedom from Great Britain.

The people of Philadelphia began then and there to celebrate our country's independence. And all Americans, everywhere, have been celebrating it ever since on Independence Day, the Fourth of July. It is a legal holiday in every state of the Union.

Independence Day was not always celebrated on July 4. Indeed, that first celebration in Philadelphia did not take place until July 8, four days after the Declaration of Independence was signed. And since in those days there were no telephones or radios or television to carry the news throughout the country, the story traveled slowly. It was two weeks before the news reached Williamsburg, Virginia— only 300 miles from Philadelphia—and the Declaration was officially announced there on July 25. But no matter just when the news reached them, the people in the colonies were proud and happy that they were part of a new nation.

In the early years of our country, Independence Day was celebrated with parades and bonfires. Ships in the harbors were decorated with hundreds of flags. Cannons roared all day and into the night. Today jet planes streak across the skies while large cities hold parades and picnics, with speeches and fireworks often part of the celebration.

LABOR DAY

Most holidays are days of rest and play, and so is this one. But it celebrates just the opposite—work!

In 1882 a man named Peter J. McGuire first proposed a legal

holiday for labor to be observed all over the United States. He was the president of the labor union called the United Brotherhood of Carpenters and Joiners of America. He suggested the first Monday in September as the date for the new holiday, and it was first observed in New York City on September 5, 1882. Five years later, Oregon made the day a state holiday. Other states soon followed Oregon's example. Today the entire country celebrates Labor Day as a legal holiday.

On this day, people have a whole day to themselves for whatever they want to do. Sometimes workers march in parades and listen to speakers who tell how important labor is and talk about ways to make better living and working conditions. Everyone enjoys the Labor Day weekend, because it is the last weekend before school starts.

COLUMBUS DAY

Christopher Columbus, the explorer who opened the Western Hemisphere to settlers from Europe, was born in Genoa, Italy, in 1451. Columbus did not set out to find a new world, or even to prove that the world is round. He believed that by sailing west he could reach the east—the rich countries of China, Japan, and India. But Columbus had no idea that our round earth is as big as it is, and he did not know that the vast continents of North and South America lay to the west between Europe and Asia.

On August 3, 1492, Columbus set out from Spain with three ships: the *Pinta,* the *Niña,* and the *Santa Maria.* The ships sailed west for seventy-two days. When at last Columbus's ship, the *Pinta,* touched the shore of an island, Columbus thought he had reached the Indies. He named the island San Salvador. San Salvador is an island in the West Indies, to the southeast of Florida. Columbus was a man of vision and courage, but to the end of his days he never realized that instead of reaching the Indies, he had discovered an entire new world.

The first celebration to honor Columbus was held in New York

This striking Labor Day poster was designed by Edward Penfield, an innovative figure in the history of American graphic arts.

City by a society called the Columbian Order. Its members erected the first public monument to Columbus on October 12, 1792. One hundred years later, President Benjamin Harrison asked the people to celebrate Columbus Day on October 12 each year. In most states, Columbus Day is now a legal holiday, and shortly before it schools have special programs based on Columbus's life.

UNITED NATIONS DAY

October 24, United Nations Day, is the anniversary of the day in 1945 when a union of nations from all over the world was formed in order to work for peace.

One of the ways in which members of the United Nations try to gain peace is by helping people in all parts of the world get enough food, good homes, good health, and education. Members of the United Nations do a great many other things, too. They help settle arguments between countries. They have started an international fund to help children whose parents cannot take care of them properly. And they have acted together to help one country that was being attacked by another.

HALLOWEEN

Of all the holidays we celebrate, Halloween, the evening of October 31, is perhaps the most fun. Yet this holiday used to be a fearsome one. Nowadays on Halloween we have parties and play games and tricks, but once it was a time of terror and grief.

Halloween was first observed long before the birth of Christ by a people called the Celts, who lived in the British Isles and northern France. They feared that when winter came, the sun they worshiped would be killed by the powers of darkness. They tried to save their god by paying a sort of tax to the forces of evil in a great ceremony on the night that we now know as Halloween. They burned some of their crops and animals in huge fires, hoping this would please the evil powers so that they would let the sun come back.

Of course, modern people know that the sun always returns. Only a few weeks after Halloween, on December 21, the days begin to grow longer, and very slowly but very surely the days begin to get warmer. The Celts, who did not know how the earth moves about the sun, thought this was because the powers of darkness had accepted their sacrifices on Halloween.

It is only in recent times that Halloween has become a holiday of fun. But even today witches and black cats and scary costumes remain as traces of the customs that were a part of Halloween during the thousands of years that it was a time of terror.

VETERANS DAY

A new holiday in the United States is Veterans Day, proclaimed by President Eisenhower on June 1, 1954, as a day "to honor veterans on the eleventh of November of each year, a day of peace." Veterans Day is observed by law in all the states, but the date has been changed to the fourth Monday in October in forty-five states. Florida, Louisiana, Mississippi, Oklahoma, and Wisconsin still celebrate it on November 11.

From 1918 until 1954, this day was observed as Armistice Day in celebration of the armistice that ended World War I. But because we have had the destruction and sorrow of war since then, it seemed more suitable to change the holiday to a day in honor of American veterans of all wars.

Today it is the custom to keep two minutes of silence at the hour when the fighting stopped in World War I. There are memorial services for the men who were killed in the wars in which the United States has fought. Special services are held at the Tomb of the Unknown (formerly Tomb of the Unknown Soldier) in Washington, D.C. An unknown American soldier who died in World War I lies buried there. Two other unknown soldiers, from World War II and the Korean War, are buried at the head of that tomb. In honoring them we honor all the brave men who fought for the United States.

ELECTION DAY

A holiday that has a most serious purpose is Election Day. On that day every citizen in the United States who has reached the age of eighteen has a chance to vote. Sometimes he or she decides on important issues. Sometimes amendments to our Constitution are voted on.

General Election Day, when congressional elections are held, is set by federal statute as the first Tuesday after the first Monday in November of every even-numbered year. The only exception is the state of Maine, which holds congressional elections on the second Monday in September. Every four years, on General Election Day, voters choose electors who in turn elect the president and vice-president of the people's choice.

Every voter plays a part in the election of the president, the vice-president, the senators, and the representatives from his state in Congress, our national legislature. In the separate states, voters also elect their chief executives and members of the state legislatures. But local elections are not always held on General Election Day. Each state sets a date of its own choice for voting on matters of local interest.

THANKSGIVING DAY

The first Thanksgiving in our land took place in the little colony at Plymouth, Massachusetts. The colonists came to Massachusetts only the year before, and in the terrible cold of their first winter in New

Although the first Thanksgiving was celebrated by the Pilgrims in 1621, it was not until 1863 that it was formally established as a holiday by President Lincoln.

England almost half their number died. Those who remained planted their small store of corn, and reaped a good harvest. They shot deer and wild turkey. They made shelters from the coming cold, and a spirit of thanksgiving was in their hearts.

Governor William Bradford spoke for all the little group when he set aside a time of Thanksgiving to God in the fall of 1621. For three days the colonists and their Indian guests sat together around the tables. They feasted and sang. They said prayers of thanksgiving. People gained new courage for the hard work they had to do.

Nowadays each year we celebrate Thanksgiving on the fourth Thursday of November, a date fixed by an act of Congress.

CHRISTMAS DAY

Probably no story in all the world is told more often, in so many ways, and in so many languages, as the story of the Nativity, the birth of Jesus Christ. This is the story of Christmas which is celebrated on December 25.

The English name "Christmas" is a shortening of Christ and Mass. In Latin the holiday is called *Dies Natalis,* the Birthday. *Noël,* the French name for this day, is taken from the Latin word *natalis.*

Christmas is a wonderful time. At no other season is there so much excitement in the air. Some of the ways in which Christmas is observed in our country are very old and some are quite new. Our houses shine with lights and decorations hung with holly, ivy, evergreen boughs, and mistletoe. Before Christmas Day thousands and thousands of cards go from friends to friends all over the earth carrying "Best Wishes for a Merry Christmas."

To small children, Christmas means just one thing: Santa Claus is coming! The Santa Claus we know can be traced to an early Christian, St. Nicholas. He was the archbishop of Myra, an ancient town in Asia Minor. St. Nicholas was a kind and generous man who gave gifts to the poor and especially to children.

The story of our modern Christmas tree lies deep in the past. The early German peoples feared and hated the freezing winters. They believed that evil spirits ran about during the dark days and long nights, trying to kill every living thing. Most of the plants and trees and bushes seemed to die, for their leaves dried and fell off, but the fragrant evergreens lived on. Men came to believe that wherever these bushes or trees were, the life-snatching spirits could not go—so they began to bring evergreens into their homes.

IMPORTANT JEWISH HOLIDAYS

The Jewish New Year is called *Rosh Hashanah.* It usually falls sometime in September. The Jews believe that on this day each year God examines a great Book of Life, in which there is a record of every act and every thought of all living persons.

Friends who meet on Rosh Hashanah say to each other, "May you be inscribed for a good year." They mean that they wish what is written in the Book of Life to be good.

In the synagogue or temple, services open with a blast on the shofar, a trumpet made from a ram's horn. From Rosh Hashanah until *Yom Kippur,* the Day of Atonement, ten days later, the people pray to God to forgive their sins.

Yom Kippur is the most solemn day of the Jewish year.

Starting at sundown on Yom Kippur Eve, devout Jews fast for twenty-four hours. (All Jewish holidays begin at sunset the evening before and last until the next sunset.) The people go to pray in the temple that evening and the next day. At sundown a long, loud sound is blown on the shofar. It is the signal that the Book of Life is closed, and a new year is beginning.

Succoth, or the Festival of the Booths, is a week of thanksgiving for the harvest and comes five days after the Day of Atonement. Many families who have yards or gardens build little outdoor booths in memory of the time during the Flight from Egypt when the Jews lived in such shelters. The booths are decorated with squashes and pumpkins, ripe corn and grapes, apples and nuts. For a week the family eats its meals in the booth.

Hanukkah is the Festival of Lights, the holiday that Jewish children love most. It comes in midwinter, usually in December. Hanukkah is the season of gift giving and parties.

This holiday is observed in memory of the time over 2,100 years ago that a brave Jew named Judah Maccabaeus recaptured the great Temple at Jerusalem, which had been taken over by the Syrians. One day's supply of holy oil—all that was left—burned miraculously in the temple lamp for eight days, until new oil could be prepared and blessed.

To celebrate this holiday, Jews light an eight-branched candlestick called a menorah. One candle is lit the first night, then one more each night until all eight are lit. The children play with a four-sided top, called a draedle, bearing the Hebrew letters N G H S. They stand for the Hebrew words that mean "a great miracle happened there" the miracle of the temple oil.

Purim is a spring holiday held in March in honor of the time long ago in the land of Persia when good Queen Esther and her cousin Mordecai saved the Jews from being killed by a wicked man named Haman. In the synagogue children shake a rattle and shout fiercely when Haman's name is said as the Bible story is told. At this time, some families have fancy dress parties, and eat special cakes.

Passover, a great holiday that celebrates the Jews' escape from Egypt in the time of Moses, usually comes in April. It begins with a festive supper called the Seder. Passover lasts a week, during which time only unleavened bread called matzoh—bread made without yeast—may be eaten. During the flight from Egypt the Jews had no time to let their bread rise, and this custom recalls that haste.

At the traditional Seder, symbolic foods are put on the table to remind the Jews of their misery in Egypt and their joy when Moses led them to the Promised Land. The youngest son of the family asks four questions about the meaning of the Seder, and the father answers him. After the story of the Seder supper has been told, the family eats a festive meal.

Passover has been celebrated continuously since Biblical times. It is one of the oldest festivals of freedom in the world.

THE HOLY DAYS OF OBLIGATION

Members of the Roman Catholic Church in the United States keep six special days called the holy days of obligation. On these days, as well as on all the Sundays of the year, Catholics are obliged to attend Mass. Special services are held in the churches.

The first of the holy days in the calendar year comes on January 1, formerly called the *Feast of the Circumcision* of Jesus Christ. In 1970 the church in Rome changed the name of this holy day to *The Feast of Mary, the Mother of God.*

The second is *Ascension Day,* in memory of the day on which Christ ascended into heaven after He rose from the dead. It is celebrated forty days after Easter.

August 15 is *Assumption Day,* a holy day to celebrate the belief that the body of Mary, the mother of Jesus, was taken directly into heaven.

The *Feast of All Saints* on November 1 is set aside by the church to honor all the saints who do not have a special feast day named for them.

The *Feast of the Immaculate Conception,* on December 8, celebrates the belief that Mary, the mother of Jesus, was conceived without original sin.

The birth of Jesus Christ is celebrated on December 25, a holy day known as the *Feast of the Nativity.*

Ethnic
Holidays in
America

Ethnic holidays are days that are celebrated or observed by groups of persons who maintain some ties to the land from which they or their ancestors have come. Since every one of us, with the single exception of the American Indians, is descended from some foreign-born ancestor, it could be said that each of us is part of some ethnic group or groups.

Some ethnic groups are far more active in preserving their national heritage than are others; perhaps many of them have only recently left the "old country" of their birth; perhaps part of their family still lives in another land; or perhaps they have become more and more interested in their old traditions, their famous men and women, their native customs and ways of life. It is the holidays that mark some of these things that we want to talk about. As you can see there are very many, and we can mention only a few here.

AMERICAN INDIAN CEREMONIES

Of course the oldest ethnic group is the American Indian, whose traditions are rooted in the very land we all share. There are hundreds of American Indian ceremonials, most of which have been performed in the same way for many decades. Perhaps you have been fortunate enough to see some ceremonial dances performed by American Indians in some regions of our country. Some you can never see, for they are sacred dances, performed in secret by members of a particular tribe or clan.

There is much variety, and at the same time a similarity, about these ceremonials. Certain ones are celebrated for definite reasons, such as the rain dance, to appeal for rain; harvest festivals, in thanksgiving for good crops, abundant hunting, or plentiful fishing. There are festivals to celebrate the time when a young boy comes into manhood; these festivals are a time of testing, similar to but not exactly like parallel ceremonies in other cultures. There are also ceremonials in praise of peace. Although in the present time tribes rarely war against each other, and there is no longer war between the

American Indian and the white man, the custom still persists in some areas of smoking a pipe, called a peace pipe or calumet, and sharing it with a former enemy or a present friend.

Ceremonies that celebrate good harvests of grain among the Plains Indians are picturesque and fanciful. Participants dress in traditional costumes with woven or painted designs that have been handed down in families; they wear high headdresses of feathers, beads, and shells. In some ceremonies masked dancers, called Katsinas, chant and dance and shake rattles made of gourds. Drums are pounded and fifes or reed pipes are played. Few Indians presently live in the middle plains, for many have moved into the cities. However, even in their urban environment some celebrations are still held in public buildings such as school auditoriums, pavilions, or stadiums.

In the southwest, where large numbers of Indians live on reservations, many ceremonies center around contests of strength or skill. Young men practice long, hard runs, in preparation for racing meets. They also have arm and neckpulling contests during which one man attempts to drag another to the earth by pulling on his opponent's arm or neck. All sorts of games are played, from table-top games of chance, played by men, women, and children, to more active games such as baseball, volleyball, and a form of stick ball. Rodeos are very popular and Indian cowboys come from great distances to compete in these spectacles. In the far north dog sled races are annual events.

A very old celebration that has lasted to the present day, particularly among some of the tribes of the northwest and Alaskan Indians, is the "potlatch." A potlatch is a big feast, usually given by a man who holds a high position in the tribe and who may be very wealthy. The feast is prepared for many guests, and food is served for several days. In order to demonstrate his wealth and high status, the host gives away many valuable gifts, and sometimes even destroys some of his possessions. Debts incurred during funeral feasts and ceremonies are sometimes paid later by a potlatch given by the remaining family.

(30)

The Zuni Indians of New Mexico
live by agriculture and are among
the finest jewelry makers in the
southwest. While the rain dance
pictured above was performed in
1900, traditional Zuni festivals
are still celebrated today.

Perhaps one of the happiest of the ceremonies is the Green Corn Dance of the Navajo, the tribe that includes the largest number of present-day American Indians. Corn dances and sun dances are held at some time of the year by most of the tribes. At some of these ceremonials beautiful paintings are made in colored sands. Sometimes these paintings are made by the medicine men of the tribe and some Indians believe they have healing powers. After the ceremonies come to an end the sand paintings are destroyed.

A day to honor all American Indians is American Indian Day on the fourth Friday in September.

DUTCH-AMERICAN FESTIVALS

Although there are Dutch-Americans living in all parts of this country, by far the largest concentration lives in Holland, Michigan, where the greatest numbers of Dutch immigrants settled. Because of religious persecution in Holland, Dutch people came to this country even before the signing of the Declaration of Independence. Celebrating their traditions with great gusto, the Hollanders each year hold a beautiful Tulip Festival, lasting several days, at the height of the tulip blooming season, usually in the middle of May. Similar smaller festivals are held in other Dutch-American communities. Many groups dress in traditional costumes. In some communities the ceremonies begin with the inspection of the streets by the mayor, who declares them to be dirty. Women carrying willow brooms and buckets of water, often hung from wooden yokes on their shoulders, proceed to scrub the streets clean. After this and at various times during the festival, there are Klompen Dances. These are dances performed by groups wearing klompen, the traditional boat-shaped wooden shoes. The sounds of the klompen can be heard in the communities all day and into the night. And there are always the tulips, Holland's special flower, to be seen and sometimes judged in special tulip contests. The days are filled with music as bands stroll along the streets and among the flower beds.

GERMAN-AMERICAN
CELEBRATIONS

German-Americans in many parts of the country, particularly in areas where there are many Americans of German descent, celebrate Von Steuben Day annually on September 17. In celebrating this day they express their pride in both their American and German heritages. Freidrich Augustus von Steuben, a German soldier, fought with the American colonists during the Revolutionary War. He served under General George Washington and was drillmaster at Valley Forge. Following the war Baron von Steuben obtained United States citizenship. The anniversary of his birth is celebrated in some large cities with big parades and dinners.

German traditions are particularly observed in some parts of the country in what are called Bavarian Festivals. They more or less follow the pattern of the festival at Frankenmuth, Michigan, usually held in June. Frankenmuth was the first home of many German settlers, who founded several agricultural villages. During the festival days traditional costumes are worn, polka (a typical German dance) bands play, and celebrants dance and enjoy sausages, cheese, dark bread, and beer such as has been served in Germany for centuries.

PUERTO RICAN-
AMERICAN FESTIVALS

In many of our large cities, especially on or near the east coast, there live groups of persons who have migrated from their homeland, Puerto Rico, a pleasant island which lies southeast of Florida. All Puerto Ricans are United States citizens since their country is a commonwealth of the United States.

Puerto Ricans who live on the mainland of the United States have many visitors from their lovely homeland for it is not very far away. Often large family groups celebrate traditional Puerto Rican festivals.

One of the floats in
New York City's
Puerto Rican Day Parade.

Some of these celebrations center around the religious holidays of the Catholic church, for Puerto Ricans are largely of the Catholic faith.

One of the favorite festivals, especially popular with children, is Three Kings Day on January 6. It is almost like a second Christmas, because on that day Puerto Rican children are given gifts and sweets. Families and friends gather to visit and exchange good wishes.

Columbus Day, the second Monday in October, is observed by many Puerto Ricans to celebrate the fact that Christopher Columbus discovered the island of Puerto Rico on his second voyage to the New World in 1493.

Perhaps the most important celebration that Puerto Ricans observe is Constitution Day, July 25. This day marks the anniversary of the signing of Puerto Rico's own self-governing constitution on July 25, 1952. The day is observed with parades, flying pennants, flags, and banners. Bands play the Puerto Rican national anthem and Puerto Ricans take pride in the self-rule that their native land enjoys.

MEXICAN-AMERICAN HOLIDAYS

The many Mexican-Americans who live in the United States feel very close to their mother country, for it is right next door! One of their most important holidays is Mexican Independence Day on September 16. In many parts of the country there are parades with bands and colorful floats. The celebration commemorates the revolution that brought about a free and independent Mexico.

Another holiday that is widely observed by Mexican-Americans is called Cinco de Mayo, which is Spanish for the fifth of May. It celebrates the defeat in 1862 of the French army of Napoleon III that occupied Mexico at that time. On the day of the celebration of Our Lady of Guadalupe, December 12, large and small statues of this patron saint of Mexico are displayed in homes and churches and are sometimes carried through the streets in predominantly Mexican-American neighborhoods.

A carnival atmosphere prevails during
the annual Feast of St. Anthony in
New York City. The Italian
celebration is enjoyed by people
from many different ethnic groups.

ITALO-AMERICAN FESTIVALS

Communities of Italo-Americans celebrate many festivals with merriment and gaiety. Many of these celebrations center around the name-days of saints. On those days, buildings, houses, and streets are strung with lights, brightly colored and lighted arches are set up, and processions wind through the neighborhoods. Often plaster images of the saints are carried on wheeled carts or floats. There is much visiting among the families of Italian descent, and much good eating of traditional Italian foods. Dancing in the streets usually ends the festive days.

Italo-Americans also celebrate Columbus Day, the second Monday in October. They take particular pride in this day, marking as it does the discovery of America by Christopher Columbus, a navigator and explorer from Genoa, Italy. Columbus's great discovery was on October 12, 1492.

They also celebrate Verrazano Day on April 17. This marks the birthday of Giovanni da Verrazano, a navigator from Florence, Italy, who explored the eastern seacoast of the United States in 1524, making the first written record of the coastline from Newfoundland to South Carolina. The Verrazano Narrows Bridge between Brooklyn and Staten Island in New York is named for him.

POLISH-AMERICAN OBSERVANCES

The many Polish-American families in this country celebrate holidays in honor of their heroes or important dates in their history. These are called commemorative holidays, and while they are not marked by joyous festivities, they are observed with quiet pride. Perhaps the oldest of these observances is that which marks the adoption of the Polish constitution on May 3, 1791. At a time when parts of Poland were being taken over by other countries, all Polish people united under their new constitution and Polish-Americans honor that unity as part of their heritage.

Americans of Polish descent observe what is called Warsaw Uprising Day, which commemorates August 1, 1944, when the people of Poland fought a heroic battle to free themselves from Nazi occupation, and to liberate Warsaw, their capital city. In this terrible battle thousands of persons were killed and Warsaw was almost destroyed. Polish people take pride in the words of President Johnson in a proclamation issued in 1964 which called this time "an exceptional demonstration of man's courage and devotion in the long and continuing struggle for human freedom."

Two famous heroes are honored by Polish-Americans and they are heroes to other Americans as well. Both men lived at about the same time and each made contributions to both Poland and the United States.

Thaddeus Kosciuszko was a Polish soldier who fought both in Poland and in our country. Sometimes he has been called the Hero of Two Worlds. He worked as an engineer during the American Revolutionary War, and among other things he built the original fortifications at West Point. For his services to this country Congress passed a special act granting him American citizenship. He later returned to Poland to fight for freedom there. A day to honor him is observed on February 10.

Count Casimir Pulaski, a Polish army officer, fought with the forces of George Washington and was wounded and died in that service. Pulaski Skyway, a portion of U.S. Highway No. 1 that is in New Jersey, bears his name. Polish-Americans have parades and memorial dinners on October 11, a date set aside by an act of Congress as Pulaski Day.

BLACK-AMERICAN OBSERVANCES

The honor of their illustrious men and women from the past until the present is one of the greatest reasons for celebration by black-Americans. Those black-Americans who fought for freedom and civil rights throughout their history are perhaps the most honored.

The best known of these is Martin Luther King, Jr., whose birth-

The late Dr. Martin Luther King addresses a
huge crowd at the 1963 march on Washington.
A year later, he received the Nobel Peace
Prize for his work in race relations.

Increasing interest among black-Americans
in their African heritage has given
rise to celebrations such as the annual
Afro-American Day parade pictured above.

day anniversary on January 15 is widely observed by Americans with different ethnic backgrounds. Black-Americans hope to have it declared a national observance. Martin Luther King, Jr. sought equal social, economic, and political rights for all minority groups, always by nonviolent methods. But his life was ended by violence when he was assassinated in 1968.

It is not possible to list here all of the distinguished men and women who preceded and succeeded Dr. King in the fight for equality and freedom. Some names stand out: Sojourner Truth, a slave, who after gaining her freedom in 1827 traveled in many states pleading for the abolition of slavery; Crispus Attucks, a hero of the Revolutionary War who was the first American killed in the "Boston Massacre" as he fought for the freedom of this country from England; Frederick Douglass, who published and preached against slavery and who was called by Abraham Lincoln "the most meritorious man of the nineteenth century"; Booker T. Washington, a famous educator at the turn of the century who taught and fought against laws that deprived black-Americans of their civil rights.

The celebrations of these persons' lives take the form of quiet ceremonies in some churches and schools. Many schools, day-care nurseries, playgrounds, and cultural centers are named for them. A monument to Crispus Attucks stands in the Boston Commons, where Crispus Attucks Day is celebrated. In some centers there are plays or dramas that depict the meaningful contributions of the lives of these persons.

Black-Americans have brought to us some of the most glorious spirituals and some of the best jazz, a form of music that they initiated. On festive family days or group celebrations there is much singing and dancing. Often such a day ends with a supper of barbecued meat and delicious cooked "greens" (leafy green vegetables), hot corn bread called "corn pone," and sweet pies. These and other appetizing dishes prepared according to traditional recipes are sometimes called "soul food" and have come to be enjoyed by many people.

A CHINESE-AMERICAN FESTIVAL

Most of the Chinese-Americans in this country live in small areas in the large cities. Their greatest festival celebrates the Chinese New Year. The date of this festival varies from year to year since the Chinese calendar is a lunar one, based on the changes of the moon, but usually falls between January 21 and February 19. In the sections of cities where many Chinese Americans live, the celebration is marked by a spectacular parade. There are brilliant floats and colorful processions of costumed people, many playing musical instruments or blowing whistles and crashing cymbals. Usually there is a tremendously long dragon who weaves from side to side, blowing flames and smoke from his nostrils. People who are watching from balconies or windows throw gifts of money wrapped in red paper and the men who are inside the fearsome dragon scramble to pick it up. Fireworks explode all through the day and into the night and the air is filled with the smell of gunpowder mingled with the spicy fragrance of joss or incense sticks. The celebration ends with banquets, payment of debts, and more fireworks.

Above: marchers in this parade, celebrating the Chinese New Year, demonstrate solidarity with their adopted homeland by donning the three-cornered hat of revolutionary times in America.

Below: In New York's Chinatown the New Year is celebrated with a week of festivities and parades in which the ceremonial dragon always makes an appearance.

These young Norwegian Americans
wear traditional costumes while celebrating
Norwegian Independence Day
in their home town in Wisconsin.

SCANDINAVIAN-AMERICAN HOLIDAYS

The Scandinavian countries of Denmark, Norway, and Sweden are represented in the United States by many groups with ties to these, their fatherlands. Although not observed extensively, there are many unique festivals celebrated by Danish-Americans, Norwegian-Americans, and Swedish-Americans. Swedish Flag Day is marked on June 6 with outdoor events and festivities to honor the Swedish flag as well as Sweden's adoption of their constitution in 1809, the oldest written constitution in all Europe. Danish Constitution Day, observed on June 5, marks the establishment of a constitutional monarchy in 1848. This form of government still exists in Denmark. Among Norwegian-Americans special pride is taken in Leif Ericsson Day on October 9. Leif Ericsson was a Norse sailor who is believed to have been the first European to set foot on the North American coast, although exactly where this landing took place has not been established.

In addition to these prideful observances each group celebrates annual festivals that reflect their heritages. One of these is the Swedish Festival. As with the others the dates may vary from year to year, as well as from place to place. Swedish-Americans try to recreate in this country many of the things they or their ancestors enjoyed in the old country. They have singing fests and concerts, play Swedish folk games, hold May Pole dances, and pitch horseshoes. There is always a smorgasbord, a large table spread with a wide variety of food—smoked, pickled, or in sauces of different kinds. Each person selects his own favorites and fills and refills a small plate. Ostakaka, lingon berries, inlagd sill, are some of the delicious dishes, with which most of us are not familiar. At some time during the festival there is a big parade with participants wearing traditional clothes.

Danish-Americans celebrate a Danish Festival sometime during the summer months. They, too, enjoy smorgasbords as well as brunches, a meal that is something of a combination of breakfast and lunch. Small bands stroll about the streets in Danish-American communities, playing concerts all day. Various outdoor sports are enjoyed. In some rural communities there are contests such as tractor pulls or plowing races.

A three-day Nordic Fest is held annually in the central part of the country, and numerous other festivals take place in several north-central states. Hundreds of Norwegian-Americans attend the festivities. There are concerts and parades and speeches by prominent persons.

AN IRISH-AMERICAN CELEBRATION

Perhaps the most well-known ethnic holiday in all the land is the favorite celebration of the Irish-Americans, the feast day of Ireland's patron saint, Saint Patrick, on March 17. Almost everywhere you look on that day you can see someone wearing "a bit of green"—a green tie, a green ribbon in the hair, a tiny artificial shamrock in the lapel. And in the large cities such as New York and Boston, where there are large Irish-American populations, huge parades are held, with marching men, women, children, and numerous bands. Sometimes entire streets have a green line painted right down the center. There is shouting and stomping and singing, and an abundance of good humor.

Since this celebration is so popular in our country it has become one of our traditional holidays, and is described elsewhere in the book.

GREEK-AMERICAN FESTIVALS

Greek Independence Day is observed by Greek-Americans on March 25, in combination with a religious holiday, the "Annunciation." Independence Day, marking the beginning of a revolt in 1821 that led to Greek independence, is widely celebrated with parades, special speeches, poetry readings, and songs. Colorful costumes from the various regions of Greece are worn by the participants. The traditional "Evzones" costume for men consisting of a short white pleated

A platoon of palace guards from Greece
were flown from their homeland to
participate in this Greek Independence Day
celebration along New York City's Fifth Avenue.

skirt, white shirt, and colored vest is worn with a "Phesi," a special type of tasseled hat. Women wear full skirts and petticoats and starched headdresses of cotton lace.

In January Greek-Americans celebrate Vasilopitta, a name that in English means St. Basil's pie or pizza. This festival is observed in churches and among families, where special pies of delicious flaky pastry, eggs, and cheese are served. Each pie contains one coin and the one who finds it in his slice is believed to be lucky the whole year long.

A festival enjoyed by shrimp fishermen and onlookers alike is the Greek-American celebration, the blessing of the shrimp fleet. This occurs on the southeastern seaboard when the shrimp fishing boats go out for the first time in the new year. Flags and pennants fly in the ocean breezes and following a blessing by an official of the Greek Orthodox Church a huge wreath or cross is thrown into the water. Coins are also flipped in by onlookers and young boys dive for them or catch them in mid-air. After the cross or wreath is retrieved, the fleet pulls up its anchors and sails away to the sound of horns tooting and whistles blowing.

*Holidays
and
Festivals
of Other
Nations*

INTRODUCTION

Countries in all parts of the world celebrate holidays. This has been true in all ages. Written histories of the people of ancient times, as well as drawings or carvings, tell us of festivals and celebrations that took place long, long before the present nations were formed. Most of these have disappeared, but some remain and are celebrated in somewhat changed forms.

Certain days that are observed by the people in the nations of today are called national holidays. Many of the national holidays commemorate some significant day in the history of the country, such as the day the nation was formed, or the birthday of some hero who helped to establish nationhood, or the day the country's independence was declared. Our own Independence Day is an example of this last.

Independence Day in the United States celebrates the adoption in July, 1776 of the Declaration of Independence. This document was ordered to be printed and distributed on that date, but was not actually signed until the following August, when fifty members of the Congress signed the parchment copy that is preserved in the National Archives Building in our nation's capital.

The declaration announced the intention of the thirteen American colonies of Great Britain to cut all their ties with the mother country, and presented the reasons why they should become independent. Although there was bitter fighting ahead for the people in the colonies during the Revolutionary War, which followed, the colonists were happy to have declared their independence and proud when they finally achieved it. How we celebrate this Independence Day anniversary is described on page 17. Other national holidays and festivals observed in this country are discussed throughout the book.

In this section we are going to tell you about how some of the other countries of the world celebrate their own holidays and festivals.

HOLIDAYS IN MEXICO

Our nearest neighbor to the south, the United States of Mexico, celebrates its national holiday on September 16. It is called Independence Day, in memory of the day in 1810 when a priest called Hidalgo issued a call to the people to revolt against their Spanish rulers and assert their independence. On this day people repeat the Grito de Dolores (the cry of Dolores), the famous plea uttered by Father Hidalgo, who has become known as the "Father of Mexican Independence." The president of the Mexican republic rings the Independence Bell, the very same bell that was tolled by the priest more than a century ago in the little town of Dolores. Actual independence from Spain did not come until 1821, after many revolutionary struggles.

The Mexican people have many festivals, called fiestas. Almost all of them are connected with their religion, which is predominantly Roman Catholic. The patron saint of every town and village is honored by a fiesta, and the largest fiesta of all of these is Guadalupe Day, December 12, in honor of the Virgin of Guadalupe, the patron saint of all Mexico.

A fiesta day usually starts with a real bang—dozens of fireworks exploding in the sky and on the ground. Little stalls are set up in the streets where people can buy special sweets or fruit juices or bright paper flowers or banners or balloons. Roving musicians called mariachis play and sing in the streets and parks. On some holidays, especially for children, a wonderful game is played with a gaily decorated article called a piñata. A piñata is a pot made of clay and covered with papier-mâché and tissue to make it into the shape of a donkey, a rooster, a rabbit, or some other animal. The pot is filled with candies and small toys. Then it is hung from a tree limb or a rafter in a house, so that it can be raised and lowered. All of the children are blindfolded. One holds the end of the rope which suspends the piñata and jerks it up or lowers it as he pleases. Each child in turn is given a big stick with which he tries to strike and

Colorful dances in regional
costumes are performed during
most local Mexican fiestas.

break the piñata. When the piñata at last is shattered, the candies and toys scatter on the ground and the children joyously scoop them up.

Small fiestas often take place in the parks and public squares. Balloons of every size and shape fly from the long poles of the balloon men; other men or women tend little stoves on which they roast chestnuts or peanuts or corn for passers-by; and there is often a puppet show to enchant the children.

CANADIAN HOLIDAYS

Our neighbor to the north, Canada, celebrates Dominion Day on July 1. It is the anniversary of that date in 1867 when an act was passed by the British Parliament permitting Canada to have dominion status under British rule. The day is marked by parades, some including the famous Royal Canadian Mounted Police in their brilliant scarlet jackets.

Canada also observes Victoria Day in honor of Queen Victoria of England, who ruled that country for sixty-four years. During that period Great Britain attained its greatest honor and achievements and the age became known as the Victorian Era.

Observance of another national holiday, Remembrance Day, takes place on November 11. Similar to our own Veterans Day, this day honors Canadian soldiers who lost their lives in the two World Wars and the Korean War, and in other conflicts where Canadian armed services were represented.

HOLIDAYS AND FESTIVALS IN INDIA

Some of the most colorful and fantastic holidays and festivals in the world take place in India. Two major national holidays are observed, Republic Day and Independence Day, but many other festivals are celebrated by most of the people throughout this vast country in southern Asia.

Independence Day on August 15 marks the day in 1947 when after many years of revolt against British rule India became an independent dominion in the British Commonwealth of Nations.

Republic Day on January 26 is celebrated in observance of that day in 1950 when India became an independent democratic republic and adopted a new constitution.

There are parades and processions in the cities on this day. The largest parade, which takes hours to pass by, takes place in New Delhi, India's capital and largest city. People from all parts of India take part in this spectacle. From remote areas come native dancers in the brilliant costumes and headdresses of their villages. Huge floats drawn by horses carry elaborate scenes from India's past, with persons dressed in authentic costumes of each era, from the time the country was ruled by Alexander the Great in the fourth century before Christ until the present day.

Dozens of gaily painted elephants march, their huge necks garlanded with flowers, their backs covered with rich velvets and brocades, their feet ringed with bells. Soldiers march or ride horses, the colors of which are evenly matched. From the deserts come the famed racing or marching camels, their riders dressed in colorful desert costumes. Balloons and banners fill the air. When night comes the city blazes with fireworks.

By far the largest part of the population in India lives in villages. Numerous holidays and festivals are celebrated in these villages in all parts of the country. The most widely observed festivals are Divali, Dussehra, Holi, and Basant Panchami. Exact dates for these cannot be given, for they are governed by the solar calendar.

Divali, held in October or November, is a festival of lights. Tiny shallow bowls fashioned of clay are filled with mustard oil or kerosene, with wicks of cotton string. Hundreds of thousands of these little lights are lighted when darkness falls. They blaze from roofs and ledges, windows and doorways, from the smallest hut in a small village to the large buildings in the big cities.

Dussehra, a word which means "ten nights," is one of the many festivals based on myths and legends. Usually held in October,

A large variety of local ceremonies
and religious rituals form part of the
daily fabric of Indian family life.
The ceremony above takes place on the
eve of the Raksha Bandhan festival.

Many Italian festivals center around
the name day of saints. This magnificent
celebration took place in Venice on the
occasion of the Feast of the Redeemer.

Dussehra depicts the story of a legendary hero who fought and destroyed a demon. In the many processions that take place there are floats where the mythical battle is fought between masked dancers. Cattle, which roam freely everywhere in India, are decorated for this occasion. Their horns are polished or painted, or capped with brass tips. Garlands and bells are hung about their necks. In some parts of the country stilt dancers join the parades. They represent the practice of some tribes of traveling on stilts across their jungle territory.

Holi is a frivolous, fun-filled holiday that takes place in late February or March. Everyone wears old clothes on this day, for by the end of the day their clothes will be dyed purple, red, green, yellow, orange, or many other colors. People who take part in this holiday fill bottles or squirt guns with brightly colored water, or they carry colored powders. They throw or squirt the water or dash the powders onto the clothing or hair of everyone they meet. It is all done in a spirit of gaiety and fun and by nightfall almost everyone is very colorfully dressed.

A day called an "Auspicious Day" is Basant Panchami, in early February. This day is a time of rejoicing because it marks the beginning of spring. It is such a good day in the minds of the people that they arrange more marriages for this time than for any other day in the year, and wedding processions can be seen in all parts, with the richly dressed bridegrooms mounted on decorated horses, and friends and followers carrying big gas-lighted chandeliers to the wedding sites. Big wedding dinners follow the marriages, often held in huge colored tents, which are rented for the occasion.

There is scarcely a day in the year when there is not a festival taking place somewhere in India.

HOLIDAY OBSERVANCES IN ITALY

The Italian Republic dates its founding from June 2, 1946. On that day the people of Italy voted to abolish the monarchy and establish a republican form of government. June 2 has become Italy's national holiday, called Republic or Constitution Day.

Parades are held in all the major cities, and fireworks are shown at night. A most unusual and brilliant procession takes place in Venice, where long lines of gondolas, gaily decorated and with banners flying, glide through the numerous canals, rivers, and waterways. Masses of people stand on the bridges and along the banks to wave and cheer. Handsome old tapestries are hung from the balconies and windows of public buildings.

The most famous festival in Italy is the Palio, held twice yearly in the city of Siena. The Palio is a horse race that takes place in the central square of Siena, the Piazza del Campo. It is a very old festival, and horses and riders are bedecked in medieval costumes and trappings. Each horse and rider represents a contrada, or district. The entire city is divided into these districts and people of each section have intense feelings and loyalties. Emotions run high during the days just before the Palio. Horses are blessed in the chapels; each contrada has a banquet; and there are parades through the twisting streets by young men in traditional costumes twirling huge banners in graceful arcs. Italians from all parts of the country, as well as international visitors, come to Siena for this exciting event.

OBSERVANCES IN WEST GERMANY

West Germany enjoys the distinction of having the oldest summer music festival in all of Europe. It was founded in 1876 by one of Germany's most famous composers, Richard Wagner, in the little town of Bayreuth. Every year Wagnerian operas are performed at the Bayreuth Festival and music lovers from the world over attend.

The German people are fond of dancing, and informal festivals are held in all parts of the country, where they dance their favorite, the polka, accompanied by the music of German bands. Often these celebrations are held in outdoor gardens, with much merriment and good cheer and an abundance of typical native food, such as their world famous sauerkraut, sausages, and cheeses.

(58)

This gigantic tent at the annual Octoberfest
in Germany provides an elaborate setting for
drinking beer and listening to music: notice
the costumed figures on the roof of the
bandstand and the facsimile of a German
village around the circumference of the tent.

October is the month of the Octoberfest—a festival originally designed to celebrate the harvest, but now a time for meeting friends, dancing, and singing. Often traditional native dress is worn. Different costumes are worn by people from the various regions in Germany. Perhaps the best known are the costumes worn by the people of Bavaria. The women dress in full gathered skirts called dirndls with several petticoats under them, so they swirl out as they dance, while the men wear short leather breeches called lederhosen and small hats decorated with feathers.

Germany's national holiday, the Proclamation of the Republic Day, is observed on June 2, with parades and speeches by the dignitaries of the cities, towns, and villages.

FESTIVALS OF SPAIN

National Day in Spain is observed on July 18 to commemorate the day in 1936 when the Spanish Civil War began. Before the rebels won this conflict Spain had had a very stormy history. The Spanish people had been ruled by many foreign conquerors, then by monarchs. They had suffered under the Inquisition, a nationwide period of intense religious persecution. When the Civil War ended in 1939 Generalissimo Francisco Franco, who had led the revolt, became dictator and the present form of government was established.

The Spanish people are proud and happy people who enjoy numerous festivals. One of their national celebrations of which they are most proud is Columbus Day, October 12, dedicated to the memory of Christopher Columbus, the famous Italian sailor who

The colorful ceremonies during
Holy Week in Seville, Spain, are
famous throughout the country.
This elaborate procession is in
honor of the Virgin of Garidad.

sailed across the ocean and discovered America, which he claimed for Spain. We in the United States also celebrate this holiday, as do many other countries in the Western Hemisphere.

Festivals or fiestas take many forms in Spain. Probably the most popular are the bull fights that are held in big arenas in the large cities. During these fiestas there are several fights between trained, tough bulls and skillful men called matadors. Matadors who perform exceptionally well become favorites of the crowds who watch, and some even become national heroes.

Religious festivals form a large part of the life of villagers. Every village has its patron saint and celebrates a special day in his honor. One of the most beautiful features of some of these celebrations is the carpet of many-colored flower petals composed by the villagers, which reaches through the main street to the doors of the church. Sometimes enormous papier-mâché figures are erected in the village square. They may be images of popular heroes or they may be used to call attention to some problem that concerns the villagers. At night these figures are burned and there are bonfires and fireworks as well. Large towns and cities have elaborate processions on special days.

NATIONAL HOLIDAYS OF RUSSIA

Russia, which is officially known as the Union of Soviet Socialist Republics, is made up of fifteen republics, with the Russian people the largest population group. They observe two major national holidays. The first, called Revolution Day, takes place on November 7 and 8. It marks the day in 1917 when the masses of people revolted against the autocratic rule of the czars.

The largest group of revolutionaries were called the Bolsheviks, now known as Communists. They seized the government under the command of their leader, a man called Lenin, and began political, agricultural, and economic reforms. These reforms were based on their political beliefs, expressed in the Bolshevik slogan, "Bread, peace, land."

A general view of Red Square
in Moscow during May Day
celebrations. The holiday is
an occasion for demonstrating
solidarity among Soviet workers.

Revolution Day is celebrated with huge parades and displays of young persons performing mass gymnastics. Similar celebrations take place on the anniversary of Lenin's birthday. The revolutionary leader is a national hero in Russia, and on both these holidays great pictures of him are carried in the processions and are displayed in homes and public buildings.

Another national holiday throughout Russia is a day that honors the working people of the land. It is held on May 1 and 2. Farm laborers, machine and factory workers, bakers, grocers—this day is a special day for all who work. Mammoth parades are held in the huge Red Square in Moscow. Flags and banners are carried by the marchers. It is customary also to parade military armaments such as tanks, rockets, and missiles.

Constitution Day is observed on May 5.

JAPANESE FESTIVALS

Festivals and holidays, called Matsuris, are a very important part of the lives of the people of Japan. Although many of these are associated with religion and often begin or end with visits to the numerous shrines, they are gay, colorful, and happy holidays. The principal national holidays are the Emperor's Birthday on April 29 and Constitutional Memorial Day on May 3.

Children's festivals are among the happiest occasions. Children's Day, a new holiday celebrated on May 5, is one of these. Boy's Day is another. On this day boys get special attention. Where there are sons the parents put up tall bamboo poles in front of their

The star festival, or Tanabata,
commemorates a legendary love story.
Colorful paper streamers
are paraded through the streets
during this popular Japanese holiday.

houses and fly huge cloth or paper fish from the tops. The cloth fish are carp, for the Japanese feel that the carp represents bravery and strength, and they expect their sons to be brave and strong. To remind their sons of these qualities, inside the houses they display ancient weapons and armor, and flags and banners which were carried by warriors in previous centuries.

A holiday for girls is the Doll Festival called Hina Matsuri. Every little girl dresses up in her party kimono and brings out her collection of dolls to show her friends. Dolls have always been important to little girls in Japan, and to their grown-up mothers and aunts, too. Throughout their lives they collect dolls, which are passed on from mother to daughter. Almost every home displays dolls representing the emperor and the empress.

Children also take part in a very old festival held twice yearly in Tokyo, the Dance of the Golden Dragon. Young men carry a huge gilded paper dragon from a shrine through the neighborhood streets. Small children carry poles with bells on them to beat time to music played on native instruments. Lanterns hang from doorways, and pots of incense perfume the air.

One of the most ancient festivals is the celebration of the anniversary of the birth of Buddha. A majority of the Japanese people are of the Buddhist faith and this important religious observance is more than 1,300 years old. People visit the numerous shrines dedicated to Buddha and carry fresh flowers to decorate them. For this reason the festival is called the Hana Matsuri or Flower Festival. Parades and processions are seen on the streets with floats and banners. Children wear headdresses of flowers, and often have their faces painted or powdered white to show they are clean and pure before Buddha.

The Sumiyomi Shrine in Osaka
is the scene of this
rice planting festival in Japan.

Japan, like many other countries, celebrates crop or harvest festivals. When the first rice is put into the rice paddies, special ceremonies are held to seek divine blessings for the crop. When harvest time comes a matsuri is held in some parts of Japan in thanksgiving. Young men in some areas parade in the streets balancing tall bamboo poles on their heads or shoulders. The poles are hung with many lanterns—sometimes as many as fifty on one pole—that swing and sway as the brilliantly dressed young men move through the crowds. The lantern-hung poles are called Kanto and the name of this festival is the Kanto Matsuri.

Japan's long history is reflected in its many neighborhood festivals. As in ancient times feats of horsemanship, archery contests, firemen performing acrobatics, processions of men or women or young boys carrying portable shrines, all have a part in one or another of the neighborhood matsuris, and in most of these traditional historical costumes are worn by the participants. Neighborhood matsuris bring a festival spirit to the very doorsteps of most of the people of Japan.

OBSERVANCES IN THE PEOPLE'S REPUBLIC OF CHINA

The People's Republic of China, on the Chinese mainland, observes National Day on October 1 and 2 to celebrate the beginning of the People's Republic in 1949. On these days thousands of schoolchildren march, shouting slogans and singing patriotic songs. Political figures make speeches and huge posters bearing photographs of the country's leaders are displayed everywhere.

China is an ancient land; its civilization is perhaps the oldest in the world. Its recorded history reaches back for more than 3,500 years. The land is the most heavily populated on earth. Its people have lived under many rules or dynasties and presently has a Communist regime. Until recently China has had very little communication with other countries and not much is known about their native festivals.

SWISS FESTIVALS

Switzerland celebrates Confederation Day on August 1. It marks a day very long ago, in 1291, when soldiers managed to free three cantons, or states, from Austrian rule. Switzerland's name is made up from the names of these three cantons—Schwyz, Uri, Unterwalder. From them, too, came the beginning of modern Switzerland, for leaders of the three original cantons signed a document known as the Perpetual Covenant in which the cantons promised to aid each other in defense against outside rule, and to fight together for freedom and independence. Switzerland became fully independent in 1646 and is one of the oldest republics in the world.

The Swiss people love music and sports and their festivals center around these. They have an internationally famous music festival each year in the city of Lucerne, and village festivals feature singing groups of yodelers or alpenhorn blowing contests. Contests in skiing, bobsledding, and mountain climbing mark the winter festivals.

FRENCH NATIONAL HOLIDAYS

Perhaps one of the most well known of all the national holidays is Bastille Day in France, which is observed throughout the country on July 14. Bastille Day marks the day in 1789 when the infamous royal French prison, the Bastille, which housed mainly political prisioners, was stormed and captured by the French people. They freed the prisoners and began to tear down the prison. Capture of the Bastille gave new heart to the people of France, who were fighting the oppressive monarchy of Louis XVI.

The revolution gathered strength and, although it lasted for ten years, it marked the end of absolute monarchies in France. Many other revolutions against authoritarian regimes in France followed, but the French people believe that the first move toward a democratic government was made on that day in 1789 when the Bastille fell. They celebrate Bastille Day with joy. There are many parades and at night the people dance and sing and shout in the streets

The Seine river in Paris
provides a beautiful setting
for this brilliant display
of fireworks—a traditional
part of Bastille Day celebrations.

until morning. An immense military procession marches down the Champs Elysée, a main thoroughfare in the city of Paris.

The French people celebrate Armistice Day on November 11 with great feeling, for France was deeply involved in the First World War, which ended with the signing of the armistice. They pay special homage to their own war dead and honor also soldiers of other nations who fought and died in France, many of whom are buried in French soil.

Other national holidays in France center largely around the religious holidays of the Catholic Church. Eighty percent of the people of France are of the Catholic faith.

HOLIDAYS IN THE
UNITED KINGDOM OF GREAT BRITAIN
AND NORTHERN IRELAND

The United Kingdom of Great Britain and Northern Ireland observes the birthday of the reigning monarch as its national holiday. The day is officially celebrated in the month of June, when the weather in Great Britain is expected to be pleasant, although the birthday may actually fall in a different month. Military ceremonies are held and regiments pass before the monarch in a colorful parade known as Trooping the Color.

Guy Fawkes Day is also observed as a national holiday in Great Britain on November 5. On this day dummies or effigies resembling Guy Fawkes are burned in public places. They are in memory of this man who was head of a band of rebels which attempted to blow up King James I and the Parliament in 1605. Guy Fawkes and his followers were trying to destroy the government because they felt the Roman Catholics in England were being persecuted. The plot to destroy the Houses of Parliament has since been called the Gunpowder Plot. Nowadays, just before each session of Parliament a mock inspection is made of the vaults below the parliamentary chambers in a traditional recognition of the belief that the gunpowder used in the plot had been concealed there.

(71)

A pleasant holiday that is celebrated throughout Great Britain, except in Scotland, is Boxing Day. This day, which occurs on the first workday after Christmas, gets its name from the old custom of filling boxes with gifts for public and private servants, tradespeople, and minor public officials. In present times money is sometimes given in place of boxes of gifts.

GREEK FESTIVALS

Greece celebrates the formation of the modern Greek nation on the national holiday, Independence Day, March 25. This marks the day in 1821 when the Greeks fought a war for independence from the Ottoman Turks, under whose rule they had lived since about 1300. Most of the observances of this day center around the military forces. In Athens, the capital, soldiers in colorful costumes parade in the central square. The palace guards, called evzones, dressed in white shirts and pleated kilts, brocaded vests, and tasseled caps, execute intricate maneuvers.

There are many festivals in Greece, most of them celebrating the patron saints of the villages. Ninety-eight percent of the Greek people belong to the Greek Orthodox Church, but although these saints' days are religious holidays they are peoples' festivals as well. The people dance and sing to the music of flutes, fifes, clarinets, castanets, and bouzoukis, stringed instruments somewhat like mandolins. Sometimes huge circles are formed, with a single performer twirling and leaping in the center, accompanied by the hand-clapping of the people in the circle. Bright traditional costumes are worn: long colored skirts and petticoats by the women, with flowing head-dresses on their heads; tight wool pants with pleated kilts over them by the men, and pleated long-sleeved white shirts, often colorfully embroidered. Lambs are roasted and eaten, and the days usually end with brilliant fireworks.

Greece is a very ancient land and has been called the "cradle of democracy" for the Greek people developed this form of government some 2,500 years ago. In its long history many, many festivals

For one day each year the men in
this northern Greek village do the
housework while the women enjoy
a holiday called Women's Rule.
This custom is rooted in the
legend of the Amazons, an
ancient tribe of women warriors.

have been celebrated. Some have continued through the ages and are celebrated in the present time.

The most well-known of these are the Olympic games, which are now held winter and summer every four years in different countries. These games are competitions between athletes from all over the world—skaters, skiers, gymnasts, wrestlers, fencers, horse-men, and many others. Water sports, racing, basketball, and volley-ball are some of the team games that take place.

Whenever they are held the Olympics open with a spectacular event. Into the large stadium where most of the games are to take place comes a racing person, carrying the Olympic torch. The torch has been lighted at Elis, Greece, on the Olympian plains, where the first Olympic games were held hundreds of years before the time of Christ. It has been carried across countries, seas, and oceans by runners or planes or ships, and is not allowed to die out. With great ceremony it is used to light the flame at the site of the new Olympic games.

NATIONAL HOLIDAYS
AROUND THE WORLD

The national holidays of the world are listed here by country in alphabetical order:

Kingdom of Afghanistan: Independence Day, May 27; Independence Festival, August 23; National Assembly Day, October 15; Deliverance Day, November 11.

People's Republic of Albania: National Holiday, November 28.

Democratic and Popular Republic of Algeria: Independence Day, July 3.

Valleys of the Andorra: Day of the Patron Saint, Jungfrau Von Meritfell, September 8.

Argentine Republic: Independence Day, July 9; Revolution Day, May 25.

Commonwealth of Australia: Australia Day, January 27.

Republic of Austria: Founding of the Second Republic, April 27; Anniversary of the Signing of the Austrian State Treaty, July 27.

Bahrain: Independence Day, August 14.

Barbados: Independence Day, November 30.

Kingdom of Belgium: Independence Day, July 21.

Kingdom of Bhutan: no known national holiday.

Republic of Bolivia: Independence Day, August 6.

Republic of Botswana: Independence Day, September 30.

United States of Brazil: Independence Day, September 7.

People's Republic of Bulgaria: Liberation Day, September 9.

Burma: Independence Day, January 4; Union Day, February 12; National Day, December 4.

Burundi: Independence Day, July 1.

Appendix

Kingdom of Cambodia: Independence Day, November 9.

Federal Republic of Cameroon: Independence Day, January 1.

Canada: Dominion Day, July 1; Remembrance Day, November 11.

Central African Republic: Independence Day, August 13; Proclamation of the Republic Day, December 1.

Ceylon: National Heroes' Day, January 1; Independence Commemoration Day, February 1.

Republic of Chad: National Day, January 11; Proclamation of Independence, August 11; Proclamation of the Republic, November 28.

Chile: Independence Day, September 18 and 19; Columbus Day, October 12.

People's Republic of China: National Day, October 1 and 2.

Republic of China (on Formosa): National Day, October 10.

Republic of Colombia: Independence Day, July 20.

Republic of the Congo: Independence Day, August 15.

Costa Rica: Independence Day, September 15; Columbus Day, October 12.

Cuba: Independence Day, May 20; Revolution Day, July 26.

The Republic of Cyprus: Independence Day, August 15.

Czechoslovakia: National Day, October 28.

Dahomey: Independence Day, August 1.

Kingdom of Denmark: National Holiday, March 11; Constitution Day, June 5.

Dominican Republic: Independence Day, February 27; National Restoration Day, August 16.

Ecuador: Independence Day, August 10; Columbus Day, October 12.

Arab Republic of Egypt: National Day, July 23.

El Salvador: National Day, September 15.

Republic of Equatorial Guinea: Independence Day, October 12; Defense of Revolution Day, November 1; Referendum Day, September 28.

Empire of Ethiopia: Emperor's Birthday, July 23; Emperor's Coronation, November 2.

Fiji: Cession Day, October 9.

Republic of Finland: Independence Day, December 6; St. John's Eve, June 23.

France: Bastille Day, July 14; Armistice Day, November 11.

Gabon: Independence Day, August 17; Armistice Day, November 11.

Gambia: Independence Day, February 18.

Federal Republic of Germany (West Germany): Proclamation of the Republic Day, June 2.

German Democratic Republic (East Germany): Liberation Day, May 8; Republic Day, October 7.

Ghana: Republic Day, July 1.

Greece: Independence Day, March 25; Panhellenic National Day, April 21.

Guatemala: Independence Day, September 15; Columbus Day, October 12; Revolution Day, October 20.

Republic of Guinea: Independence Day, October 2; Defense of Revolution Day, November 1.

Guyana: Independence Day, May 26.

Republic of Haiti: Independence Day, January 1.

Republic of Honduras: Independence Day, September 15.

Hungarian People's Republic: Liberation Day, April 4; Constitution Day, August 20.

Republic of Ireland: St. Patrick's Day, March 17; Republic Day, June 17; Anniversary of Proclamation of the Republic, June 17.

Republic of India: Republic Day, January 26; Independence Day, August 15.

Indonesia: Independence Day, August 17.

Iran: Birthday of the Shah, October 26; Constitution Day, August 5.

Republic of Iraq: Republic Day, July 14.

State of Israel: Independence Day, April 23; National Holiday, May 11.

Republic of Italy: Founding of the Republic, June 2; National Unity Day, November 4.

Republic of Ivory Coast: Independence Day, August 7.

Jamaica: Independence Day, first Monday in August.

Japan: Emperor's Birthday, April 29; Constitution Day, May 3.

Hashemite Kingdom of Jordan: Independence Day, May 25; King's Coronation, March 8; King's Birthday, November 14.

Republic of Kenya: Independence Day, December 12.

State of Kuwait: National Day, June 19.

Kingdom of Laos: Independence Day, July 19.

Republic of Lebanon: Independence Day, November 22.

Kingdom of Lesotho: Independence Day, October 4.

Republic of Liberia: Independence Day, July 26.

Libyan Arab Republic: Independence Day, December 24.

Principality of Liechtenstein: Religious national holidays associated with observances of the Roman Catholic Church.

Grand Duchy of Luxembourg: National Day, June 23.

Malagasy Republic: Independence Day, June 26.

Republic of Malawi: Independence Day, July 6.

Malaysia: Independence Day, September 16.

Maldive Islands: Independence Day, July 26.

Republic of Mali: Independence Day, September 22.

Malta: Independence Day, September 21.

Islamic Republic of Mauritania: Independence Day, November 28.

Mauritius: Independence Day, November 28.

United States of Mexico: Independence Day, September 16; Columbus Day, October 12; Anniversary of the Revolution, November 20.

Principality of Monaco: National Fete, November 19.

Mongolian People's Republic: Constitution Day, June 30; Mongol Revolution Day, July 11.

Kingdom of Morocco: Independence Day, November 18.

Republic of Nauru: Independence Day, January 31.

Nepal: Constitution Day, December 16.

Kingdom of the Netherlands: Queen's Birthday, April 30.

New Zealand: National Holiday, February 6.

Republic of Nicaragua: Independence Day, September 15.

Republic of the Niger: Republic Day, December 18.

Federal Republic of Nigeria: Independence Day, October 1.

Northern Ireland: St. Patrick's Day, March 17; Orangeman's Day, July 12.

Democratic People's Republic of North Korea: no known holiday.

Kingdom of Norway: Constitution Day, May 17.

Sultanate of Oman: no known national day.

Islamic Republic of Pakistan (West Pakistan): Pakistan Day, March 23.

Republic of Panama: Independence from Colombia, November 3.

Republic of Paraguay: Independence Day, May 14.

Republic of Peru: Independence Day, July 28.

Republic of the Philippines: Independence Day, June 12.

Polish People's Republic: Liberation Day, July 22.

Portuguese Republic: Day of Portugal, June 10.

Rhodesia: Independence Day, November 11.

Socialist Republic of Rumania: Liberation Day, August 23.

Republic of Rwanda: Independence Day, July 1.

Republic of San Marino: Anniversary of the Founding of San Marino, September 3.

Kingdom of Saudi Arabia: National Day, September 23.

Republic of Senegal: Independence Day, August 20.

Sierra Leone: Independence Day, April 27.

Republic of Singapore: National Day, August 9.

Somali Democratic Republic: Independence Day, July 1.

Republic of South Africa: Republic Day, May 31.

People's Democratic Republic of Southern Yemen: Independence Day, November 29.

Union of Soviet Socialist Republics: Constitution Day, December 5; October Revolution, November 7 and 8; May Day, May 1 and 2.

Spain: National Day, July 18.

Republic of the Sudan: Revolution Day, October 21.

Kingdom of Swaziland: no known holiday.

Kingdom of Sweden: King's Birthday, June 2.

Switzerland: Confederation Day, August 1.

Syrian Arab Republic: Evacuation Day, April 17.

United Republic of Tanzania: Independence and Republic Day, December 9.

Thailand: His Majesty's Birthday, December 5.

Republic of Togo: Independence Day, April 27.

Kingdom of Tonga: no known holiday.

Trinidad and Tobago: Independence Day, August 31.

Republic of Tunisia: Independence Day, March 20; Republic Day, July 25.

Republic of Turkey: Freedom and Constitution Day, May 26 and 27.

Republic of Uganda: Independence Day, October 9.

United Kingdom of Great Britain: Boxing Day, December 26.

United States of America: Independence Day, July 4; others discussed in book.

Republic of Upper Volta: Independence Day, August 5.

Eastern Republic of Uruguay: Independence Day, August 25.

Vatican City: Religious holidays only.

Republic of Venezuela: Independence Day, July 5.

Democratic Republic of Vietnam (North Vietnam): no known holiday.

Republic of Vietnam (South Vietnam): Anniversary of the Revolution, November 1.

Independent State of Western Samoa: no known holiday.

Yemen Arab Republic: National Day, September 26.

Socialist Federal Republic of Yugoslavia: Republic Days, November 29 and 30.

Republic of Zaïve, former Democratic Republic of Congo: Independence Day, June 30.

Republic of Zambia: Independence Day, October 26.

Aschauffler, Robert Haven. *The Days We Celebrate*. New York: Dodd, Mead, 1940.

Describes celebrations for special occasions in the United States.

Dobler, Lavinia. *Customs and Holidays around the World*. New York: Fleet Publishing, 1962.

This book shows how various faiths and religions have influenced holiday observances in many countries.

Douglas, George William. *The American Book of Days*. New York: H. W. Wilson, 1938.

Information concerning American holidays and anniversaries and notes on Christian and Jewish observances.

Fenner, Phyllis Reid. *Feasts and Frolics*. New York: Alfred Knopf, 1949.

Contains special stories for various holidays.

Gaer, Joseph. *Holidays around the World*. Boston: Little Brown, 1953.

Describes the pageants, games, gifts, and symbols used by people in different lands as they celebrate their festivals.

Johnson, Lois S. *Happy New Year around the World*. Skokie, Ill.: Rand McNally, 1966.

Tells of the ways particular countries celebrate the new year.

———— *How Birthdays are Celebrated Round the World*. Skokie, Ill.: Rand McNally, 1963.

Descriptions of birthday celebrations in twenty-four different countries.

Larrick, Nancy, comp. *Poetry for Holidays*. Champaign, Ill.: Garrard, 1966.

Poems by various authors describe many of the holidays we celebrate in the United States.

Bibliography

Sechrist, Elizabeth Hough. *Red Letter Days,* rev. ed. New York: Macraw Smith, 1965.

Tells the origins of holidays and the customs of observing them around the world.

Weber, Susan Bartlett, general ed. *Crowell Holiday Books.* New York: Thomas Y. Crowell.

A series of well illustrated books that provide introductory material on United States holidays and religious holidays for younger readers. Titles are:

Arbor Day, Aileen Fisher, 1968.

Christmas, Barbara Cooney, 1967.

Columbus Day, Paul Showers, 1965.

Easter, Aileen Fisher, 1968.

Election Day, Mary Kay Phelan, 1967.

Flag Day, Dorothy Les Tina, 1965.

The Fourth of July, Mary Kay Phelan, 1966.

Halloween, Helen Borten, 1965.

Hanukkah, Norma Simon, 1966.

Human Rights Day, Aileen Fisher and Olive Rabe, 1966.

Indian Festivals, Paul Showers, 1969.

The Jewish New Year, Molly Cone, 1966.

The Jewish Sabbath, Molly Cone, 1966.

Labor Day, James Marnell, 1966.

Lincoln's Birthday, Clyde Robert Bulla, 1965.

May Day, Dorothy Les Tina, 1967.

Mother's Day, Mary Kay Phelan, 1965.

New Year's Day, Aliki, 1967.

Passover, Norma Simon, 1965.

Purim, Molly Cone, 1967.

St. Patrick's Day, Mary Cantwell, 1967.

St. Valentine's Day, Clyde Robert Bulla, 1967.

Skip around the Year, Aileen Fisher, 1967.

Thanksgiving Day, Robert Merrill Bartlett, 1965.

United Nations Day, Olive Rabe, 1965.

Washington's Birthday, Clyde Robert Bulla, 1967.

Index